BREATHING WATER

BREATHING WATER

Meditations on the Plain and the Profound
A book of poems

Cathy, it's been so great to see
you again!
Marina
May 25/13

MARINA MARTIN

To order additional copies of this book, contact:
Xlibris Corporation
1-888-795-4274
www.Xlibris.com
Orders@Xlibris.com
105170

CONTENTS

Acknowledgements...9
Introduction..11
On a Seed Packet...14

Chapter 1: Original Cry..15
     Gone...17
     Intrusions..18
     Gulls...19
     Insouciance...20
     Animal Eye..21
     Bell on the Dunes...22
     Laura...23
     Dasein..25

Chapter 2: Seeing Them...27
     Salig Lut...29
     The Photographer..30
     The Goose...31
     The Fox...32
     Tree Frog...34
     Grotto..35
     Spring Dog..37

Chapter 3: Holding In The Light..39
     Holding in the Light..41
     The Vase..43
     High Noon...45
     On The Edge...46
     Berry Picking...48
     Latent Image..49
     Papa..50
     Sally...52
     Zygote..53
     Pantheon..55

Chapter 4: Being There 57
    One Moment...59
    Patagonia Ice Field 60
    Helen 61
    La Cloche Silhouette 62
    Burnished..64
    Pis Aller..65
    Pachelbel's Hope..66
    Offering to the Unseen 68
    Mother, Goddess Reaping 69

Chapter 5: Gathering Strands...71
    Essences..73
    Belladonna 74
    Groundling 75
    Breathing Water 76
    Call-Note 79
    Between...80
    Final Flight 81

About the Author..83
Vale in the Dunes..84
You May Touch this Poem 85
Artist's Statement 87

for my husband Trevor,
our children Hugh, Alex, Laura and their families

ACKNOWLEDGEMENTS

This is a book of lived experiences, some my own, some my reactions to those of others, perhaps a few of these my readers. My first acknowledgement, therefore, goes to you, the reader, as a participant in this endeavour. For those of you who are not typically readers of poetry, I hope you will find time to listen mindfully to the words, the sounds of them. If a poem shakes you or stirs you, if you wonder at its intent or if the leaps in meaning seem long, it is my hope that you will re-read, exploring your personal experience of what the words may hint at in context of the particularities of your own life. You are welcome to, and I hope you will enjoy these poems on whatever level of interpretation touches you, from sound and image and your connections with the natural world, to discoveries held in metaphor and veiled identity.

I again acknowledge my family, to whom this book is dedicated. As early readers, they have given me the love and encouragement to see it to fruition. My daughter Laura, in addition to her support and advice, has offered black and white copies of her magically colored blind-touch paintings for this book, and a color image for its cover, as well as several pencil illustrations from her thesis, *In Media Vita*.

A very special person in the making of this book is Adam Getty, who has generously worked as my editor, and who over the past few years has been a kind critic. Adam has a clear understanding of my work, and at times seems to grasp the subliminal material that enters my writing, better that I do.

Many thanks also to Carolyn Smart of the *Writing With Style* program at the Banff Centre, who has provided fine advice and whose encouragement prompted me to compile this collection.

A number of my poems have evolved through daily meditations and readings, or through weekly meditation with a group of friends in West Hamilton, to whom I am much indebted for their insights and wisdom.

Finally, I am forever grateful to my friends at the Hamilton Poetry Centre, some of them my instructors in the McMaster University/Mohawk College Certificate of Writing program, and I offer particular thanks to Marilyn Gear Pilling, Bernadette Ryan, Linda Frank and again, Adam Getty. They have provided ongoing, thoughtful training and comment in the art of language, and have shared their deep knowledge both in workshops and by example.

Marina Martin

INTRODUCTION

I have read somewhere that Canada has the highest proportion of its people writing poetry of any country at any place and time. While much of that writing is superficial, this fact might be interpreted to mean that poetry is for Canadians a kind of journal writing. In fact, most poetry is probably just that, if we think of journals as recording the events and impressions of our days, but also our thoughts about them. In my estimation the poetry of Marina Martin refines this activity to its highest form: the examination of a life bears witness to it but also redeems its dark moments through reflection.

And reflection, more than anything else, is what we have here. For Marina's poems often start with some difficulty the narrator is facing only to be distracted by external phenomenon, such as the landscape in "La Cloche Silhouette". Yet to call it distraction is perhaps perverse, for the possibility exists that the difficulties themselves are distractions and that the poet is actually returning to the heart of the matter, and situating her desire within it. This interplay between self and universe is fraught at times with singularity, as in the poem "Pantheon", but it is this departure from the familiar that is the mark of truly original writing.

Marina's work often reminds me of Darwin's conclusion to perhaps the most controversial nature poem ever written, The Origin of Species, when he points to "elaborately constructed forms, so different from each other, and dependent upon each other in so complex a manner" before continuing on to say: "There is grandeur in this view of life". I resurrect Darwin only to say that Marina's poetry can be looked at from one perspective as providing a coherent vision of existence as experienced by one person, but at a remove from such intellectual processes it becomes clear that this vision is the result of disparate and seemingly unconnected moments being gathered together in the unnatural form that is a book of poetry.

I am honoured that Marina invited me to participate in putting together the collection as it stands now, but there are many other ways of looking at her poems. I'd like to join with her in inviting you to disassemble what you find here and rebuild it in different combinations. There is no heart of the matter . . .

Adam Getty

Adam is this year's winner of the Hamilton Arts Award for Literature

ON A SEED PACKET,
received in the mail, Saas Fee, Switzerland

"I send you the sweet germ of my intensity
to root in the loam of a land unknown to me.

I send you the heart of the germ of my intensity
locket of abundance crafted in a land of antiquity.

I send you the courage of the heart of the germ
of my intensity, supple as golden barley blown,

bearing wisdom of genomes, invisible
in their innerness, given to divisions."

I

ORIGINAL CRY

GONE

With my dream in his talons
the owl has flown away into the forest
into a deep tangle of trees. What
do I do with the dark, dark nights
when the milky way pivots obscured,
phantom cast of cumulus drifting before?
What do I do, when cusp of a quarter moon
tips empty like the by-gone day?
When sleep evades where do I put my hands
who have lost their grasp, my feet
seized in their fleeing?

Gone the warm dream
where hands and feet tingled, dream
curled near the fire, dream in long grasses
by the slough, dream of listening together
for the owl—long whinny of screech owl
carried across tree-lines on breathless nights.
Gone the passing dream of train rides,
car rides, fields a-blur with arrivals.

Even the landscape dreamed for me,
and swallows, heads tucked beneath wings.
Wood creatures gathered gifts in their sleep,
deep chests heaving, legs a-flutter:
pieces of broken stone, bones,
fall flowers of witch-hazel, seed of thistle,
a loose tuft of whitening hair.
                              All gone.
I keep searching for the owl to return
and settle on his perch, in benediction
folding low his fringed wings.

INTRUSIONS

What shall I do
with the hand that beseeches,
reaching up from duckweed pond
where remnants of the disappeared
linger, grappling for my wrist?

What shall I do with those feet
pacing the ceiling, that burst
through yellow lath, toes dangling?
What shall I do with a knife that lodges
in the wall over my head,
the whir of it?

And what shall I do
with this endless glacier forever advancing,
right here in the brine of fiords,
deep within every flaw-lead?

Just—suchness—is what I long for,
just—being in every moment,
touching each—just
somewhere in the declination
between magnetic north
and true north—just
anywhere.
            Only
my un-self: thought-less,
enthralled, part of trees in fall,
part of dissipating clouds,
a wave in a wide ocean
of waves, everywhere green-blue
and broad open sky.

GULLS

In a late dusting of snow,
gulls hover and glide
above an April field newly opened
to the plough. They spiral
through a wash of pale gray,
reeling in synchrony, all cohered
by unseen hands
                    that sweep the sky

and the infinite knowing
of deeply secret strips below
—the rows of steaming sod
turned onto fresh snow—
that will feed their craving,
will in the end consume,
drawing sky and fowl
and the man with his plough
inside their reflective bed,
already counterpart
to the endless circling overhead.

INSOUCIANCE

The emptiness of awareness
has arrived, leaving room
                    for rare things:

a ray of sun,
filtered through mist and half-closed eyes,
its inner flicker of fire;

clarity of the sparrow's last farewell;

a delphinium that blooms through November,
strands of pale blue perfume hanging;

turn and curl of golden leaves sifting
into umber slather of earth;

raspberries, plumpness rolled
on the tongue after the first hard frost;

blind prick of thistle that near the hedgerow
feeds a clutch of ruby-crowned kinglets;

a hazel-eyed child who peers
beneath the names of things,
fingers and tastes them all;

for every gift that was never grasped.

Like a cupped hand
the emptiness of awareness absolves,
and all is allowed to spill
                    through the fingers.

ANIMAL EYE

Out of the knot glows an animal eye,
as an ember glimmers there.
                              Placid.
Faint. Fluid as a pine in the wind
swaying, everywhere gazing.
                              Patient.
Alive within resilient wood
over eons silently gleaming.
                              The eye
rests, content, limp body in its jaw,
lovingly holds it.
                    Sees me,
knows I am here. For now satiated,
waits, listening,
                    one day
to spring from depths of severed rings,
                    fire
in its glow,
            ears flat,
                    jaw open.

BELL ON THE DUNES,
'S-GRAVENHAGE

Have you heard the ancient cadence
of whales, slow as grinding
of continental shelves, deep
as depths of shipwrecks? Here,

on shoulders of the dunes, on blown sands
tinged with sublime blue, the wind whips,

makes mockery of the colossal, changes it,
its solitudes, its raiment of endangered grasses.

Have you heard the gong, the great cast bell
set long ago upon the Lowland dunes?

Have you heard it tolling,
in consolation stroking the air,

still admonishing the gray deserted
bastions—remnants of a great war, left standing
in the sands—its summons swelling
in synchrony with the low groan of whales?

LAURA

The first I knew of you
was a soft cry, flutter
of firefly wings in my ear.
Here, you shelter still,
curled round the anvil
and hammer of my hearing.
My ear a map of our lives,
relief of hills and valleys
traveled, a place of song
and whisperings, where tuned
to the arcing moon in her path,
we listen to things of the world:
earth, metal, wood, water,
whir of the open fire,
                    night.

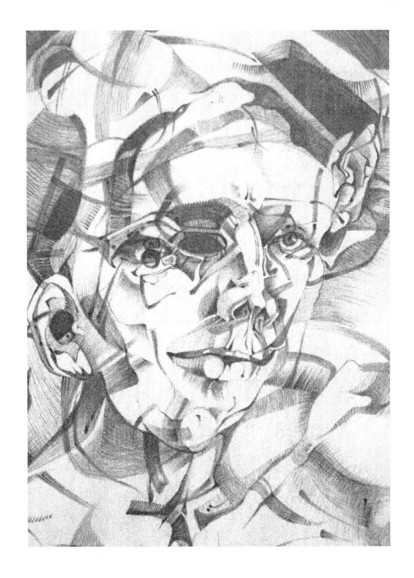

DASEIN,
"BEING THERE"

Singing
deep in the throat
we meet in music. Palm
to palm, speaking with hands
we flutter between, absorb
light and shadow (ourselves
reflected in eyes)
Absolved.

Dasein
in space and time
we pass through one another
like water, hum refrain within
ancient kettle-stones of our being,
alike forever changed, etched
into hollow of softened lime, echoes
rising—tongues tremulous
deep in the throat.

II

SEEING THEM

SALIG LUT, "BLESSED FOLK"

They come into being
and leave. I hear song,
soft footsteps in snow, dim
the light, so not to frighten folk
that rise from the highest pasture
      where the northern harrier flies.

Unfinished seekings
of the dead apprehend
and I, compelled to answer,
atone with half-closed eyes and ears
that hear and see their voice and form of being.
This place has outlived them:
voles scurry beneath old meadow snows,
thorn and dogwood, seeded deep,
      finger hidden abodes.

With rhyme and dance
they pour long-side my lodging:
they know two souls reside inside of me,
that I have need to breach the past,
release the hour and minute of this night,
leave shelter of low-slope roof
and double doors: they call
for me to follow, as pthalo shadows
leap through guttering light,
and prints in drifts of winnowed snow
recede to a place where wind
      and trees outlive me.

THE PHOTOGRAPHER

On the far side
of the field, low angled sun
throws gold upon a stand
of aspens that shiver
around a few in-filling oaks
beneath a huffle of scattered russet,
the great seed-tree revealed
as it undresses.

And before this,
unlit but for a silver plume here and there,
dull buff of the wild meadow
slipping into its thick
winter woolies.

Everything
stands in transient shades
of readiness.

Yet I
all the long evening
have this restless feeling,
long for my son, the photographer.

THE GOOSE

Fat upended goose
dabbles upon a flat expanse of stillness
in the gray morning.
She has seen the ultraviolet light
shake like a veil of rain
across the lake.

The others gather
to the lee of an outcrop, a racket
of calls and honks in shoreline reeds,
all streamlining feathers, all
facing the same way.
Only the fat goose fails to heed
the oncoming squall, as she seeks
another tender shoot.

Then scooped by a sudden burst
and upward current of sleet,
and a howl that flattens long offshore grasses,
she disappears into a whirlwind of white,
wings twisted inside out.

        A year and six months later
she reappears, retrieves her mate
from his new love. After the scuffle
she uncovers a displaced egg
which, tap by tap, she rakes
with her green beak and arched neck
into the quilt of her down,
as she settles her plumpness
over his stick nest.

THE FOX

"Don't shoot 'til you see
the whites of his eyes,"
they had said.
Last time, he had taken flight
just as I blundered upon his crime.
Now I was waiting for him,
waiting, and there he came, hesitating,
        one step at a time.

Hands on new-blued barrel, cold,
cold and blue upon the trigger,
I shivered, then remembered
little Sally Henny-Penny,
how her plumage gleamed,
and now one feather in her nest—
        my darling chestnut Banty hen!

And double-tufted Crop-Top, too,
how he lay contorted, flapping—
never having learned to fly.
Now the fox was out of luck,
for I was waiting, and I had him
in my sights as he came forward,
        hesitating.

His eyes were gleaming amber,
and I could see him well:
how sleek he was, how thick
his reddish fur and tail,
how calm his eyes,
the whites just barely showing.
He stopped and stared, and I could tell
       there was no malice in his look

but in his gaze a gathering, a scrutiny
and deep within an inquiry.
So then I questioned in my mind,
just what was my intent. I stood
upright and lowered arms,
quite mesmerized behind the barn,
       as he held motionless.

The moment that I eased he turned
and loped away in easy stride, sleek body
coursing side to side, his dense tail spreading,
tipped in white. He stopped just once,
seemed unconcerned,
       then through the brush
           bobbed out of sight.

TREE FROG

His high-pitched trill ascends
the evening air—long, surprising
for such a little one as this.

Tiny cups on each translucent toe,
oozing wetness, suck his being
into the folds of the being
that is the tree that shelters him.
There he clings, still of a sudden,
cold skin soft, metallic,
a green sheen that shines
            unearthly.

GROTTO

We inhale dampness
feel the vibration of mating songs:

banjo of green frogs
clack of mink frogs
long-held groan of toad
all in mossy drip of humidity.

We quiver
with rouse of tree-top cicadas,
friction of wings,
and over and over the rub of legs.

We become
ground-singing crickets,
or hooked-tip moths
pulling our oars across leaves.

With echoed staccato we enter
our perennial selves,
a forbidden grotto.

SPRING DOG

Flying none-the-less
he flaps the wind with his ears,
sprouts wings from his long legs,
ascends currents high above
the downward spirals of mating snipe.

He doesn't know what he is,
forever follows braying geese
into never-worlds. Always his nose seeks,
beyond our own grasping, after the truth.

Should he range too far into forest depths,
should he lose his way, he bears a tag and chip,
and in any case we can hear his red bear-bell
as he descends through soundless growth
of mouse-eared leaves of maple and oak.

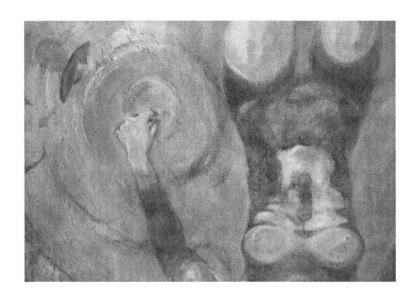

. . .my mind is absent

III

HOLDING IN THE LIGHT

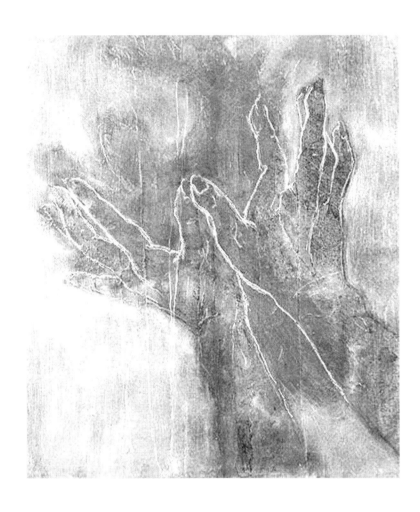

HOLDING IN THE LIGHT

I leave my thoughts at your back door,
slide over the surface of being here,
in passing apprehend the sway
      of a rose in the breeze.

What would you call the color of this rose?
Soft peach, on fringe
of whiteness? A pallor so warm
      it can be caressed in the hand.

I open every moment, gather
your words, begin to dress your wounds
with rose petals layered one atop another,
      one-third overlapping each.

THE VASE

Tonight the glass is fuller than with flower.
I cannot enter it but for my gaze,
transparent black, its shadows seem a bower
that shelter from an ever-growing maze.
The water flows, where from I cannot say,
so let it wash and wander where it may.

Black, black! My mind's confusion is a widow
that stalks within her web the lowly moth
who, fluttering, has entered through a window
and landed on a multicolored cloth—
a frightened figure on uncharted ground
in search of flame that nowhere can be found.

But there! There glimmers a reflection:
midnight moon lies deep within the glass.
The vessel holds the image to perfection—
beneath moon's glow, the limpid waters pass.
I climb a straggling fern up to the brink,
where poised in limen, I could rise or sink.

I look above and see the black, black widow
with all her legs and many-mirrored eyes,
and there beyond, the breeze has closed the window
and far below, the moon begins to rise.
I chose my fate before the day's begun,
and slip into illumed oblivion.

HIGH NOON

In this unforgiving brilliance,
Shadow, where are you hiding?
                              You,
Shadow, who skirts undersides of leaves,
who travels the western face of a tangled field
and flits beneath webs draped from milkweed
        and long reed-canary grasses.

Deepest Shadow, where are you now?
Do you see them—the snakes?
Are they sunning by the scrub?
        Are you listening, do they rattle?

Shadow, I have need of you,
                        you
who would whisper to willing ears, unfold
subdued truths and expose
simmering embers beneath the ash,
you, who would leap
from wild sedges screaming rape!
strangulation! and more, much more, weep
        for the burning away of fingertips!

Shadow, I mean you, the one
who follows me, precedes me, upon whom
I daily tread, whom I ignore, flee from, dread,
                              yes you,
Shadow—I have need of you today.

ON THE EDGE

The edge of terror
hones itself on a whet-stone
set upon the shelf, where memory fills
a hollow jug that stands long-side,
so very still—it starts to teeter
on the sill, to tremble, tip,
release, then flow in stream of red
to the floor below

and I cannot run—
my feet are bound, and I cannot scream
or make a sound
as the forethought of the things I dread
emolliates the fearful red

upon my wrist
a hand clasped tight, trap-door
in the closet that gapes at night, a knife
on the table, a stain on the floor
and I cannot leave them lying there
but hide them, hide them
far from the bed, for they embellish
the awful dread. I latch the cupboard,
scrub the floor, place the knife
outside the door

then pour a tub for tortured womb
in the water I lie with hidden wounds
and the water is warm
and music plays soft, so leaving my body
I hang from aloft
as I slash with a razor
again and again and it's all very easy
and really no pain

and perfume of heather
carries me home to a church
by the river, with tapestried dome
(so patiently stitched by women like me)
where light slides aslant across the brocade,
over back-lit trees and birds in the shade.

BERRY PICKING

There is a price for this lush fruit: swollen,
clustered on thorny canes, ready to devour,
inhale, to press to lips in the picking.
Lower still you seek, an ample sweetness
beneath leaves drooping over berries,
rich, half-hidden, that ooze
crimson juice in the hand.

You reach deeper,
                    cry out at sudden sting

of a wasp, and stab of canebrake—
long naked trails over pale arms retreating
that tear, redden, scar.

There is more,
            you want more.

Desire draws you into an inner thicket,
shade of split stems and spines that twist
and you bleed deep redolent streams
as your fingers reach
for thick drifts
                of dark hair curling.

LATENT IMAGE

The photograph lies, of course:
he stands firm, smiling, muscled hands
upon her weightless shoulders,
blue eyes gray in aged monotone print.
Pallid black and white hides pain,
its colors, blanches
the strawberry blonde of her hair.
She smiles on command,
a still endearing smile that lends a sheen
to the un-lovely

She remembers remembering,
which may not be the same
as the real thing—that has grown old—
or, even the last time she recollected it:
it hurts anew, down deep,
somewhere indescribable,
somewhere tribal

The photo shifts, blurs, still denies the truth:
the furtive theft of color, of tone,
layer by layer

PAPA
(for Teunis van Heteren)

He was only there for a little while
not long enough, really, to grow familiar.
He recalls digging through deep dura
of gray clay, tunneling like a vole,
with rose-webbed hands
and pale nose like a zinnia
      going to seed.

The diffuse amber glow,
soft skylight of sundown,
      he never reached.

He came back when he heard me call
"Papa!" He would have been content
to be reclaimed, he said,
to the warm convoluted earth
that knows things beyond his reckoning,
but he wanted to touch me
      one more time.

SALLY

Something about the child, born
with all she needed to know, primed
by outpourings of love, primped
with a single perfect curl. Something
about the monochrome blue-gray eyes:
a still sort of adoration
that holds her as she was—even now.

Sally searches the eyes—her own—over
and over. The child had posed so, before
her father left when she was five years old,
before her sadness subtracted
from what she knew. She hoped
she could make things better,
yet still she waits.

*

Where does it come from, such desire,
such longing, in a new person:
this resounding of shingle combed
by curling waves in retreat, azurine
echoes reverberating stone to sky,
this purity of gray-blue cosmos
barely etched upon, that refuses
to be etched upon?

Within these eyes
she sees the infant hope, dying
to be born, withholding still
the long squawk of possibility.

ZYGOTE

Deeper than desire, this:
a return to the womb, a letting.
A curling of hands and feet
drawn back through the moist passage,
a slipping into time before choice.

To release all,
diminish into the ardour
of a single sperm and ovum,
so to remain forever fused,
with shared hands and feet
like seaweed waving—

to swim with you into the depths
of this green ocean.

PANTHEON

The road licks me on along
long lines of yellow—wet russet tongue
sliding over a shoulder of the hill.

An immense eye sets upon me here,
with ardour gathers me in: sphere
of lustrous sun, the ancient god
waiting to consummate.

An eagle swoops low, soars,
wings spreading before the orb:
a fringed lid folding.
                        Recognizing him,
I give myself up to his wild cry
and rise to become the scream.

IV

BEING THERE

ONE MOMENT

Cross-legged
on the edge of a gully
I run my fingers over face, arms, knees
touch my tongue to saline
of upper teeth

feel the fibers
      of a lambs-wool sweater
            pulled high to my ears
      inhale
the gray of passing rain.

Strange . . .
        nothing at all has changed.
Yet
I have just beheld
a rainbow sweeping hillsides
for a single boundless moment.

PATAGONIA ICE FIELD

Nothing
has ever remained the same:
stasis of days and weeks
an illusion.

        Over eons the ice
          has shifted lichened boulders,
forever undercutting ancient layers
of moss and contortions
of aged cypress.

        Without warning
          a gale from the west,
now only roots protrude
through the whiteness.

        From beneath bleached sheets
          grasping at anything, unable
to enunciate—your hand.
So slowly it happened suddenly.

HELEN

I only met her in images:
she was a long time gone
when I came along.

There she was, atop a mountain
a rosy glow, arms waving spun luminosity
like fine streams of lava,
and I knew
    she was of the earth.

She descended and stretched,
a tree by water's edge, arms
swinging in ripple-bands between
the clear pools, her reflection more perfect
than she remembered herself to be,
and I knew
    she was of the water.

Closer she ventured, settling,
a broad leaf blanket-stitched upon my day,
and I knew
    she was of simple, living things.

LA CLOCHE SILHOUETTE

The rock senses my standing
in this barren landscape,
on this broad span of igneous scored
by bands of jagged quartz:
I hardly feel lonely though alone.
In its transilience,
in its abiding memory
it grows layers—this strange
rose strata—and of a sudden
conjures Carmichael,
Carson, Jackson, Lismer.
As they gather beside me
the landscape
       transpires to a work
             of the mind.
Here,
we dig hidden veins
for our myths,
each in our apartness
becoming part of this sheer geology.
The masters in transit span
adamant jutting granite
to the finer lines of horizon
(only slightly less tortuous)
       beneath pale gray haze
           and they are gone.
Alone
once more
with rock and water,
my body gapes as their mass sinks
into interstices of tendon and bone,
       and the ache amasses . . .

the ache,
and traveling deeper,
low visceral pain
in happening upon a valley
where boughs and deadfalls lie crossed:
curved portals to innerness gesture
into demiurgic world of burls, hollow trees
(whose arms reach inside themselves),
amber-olive mosses, Showy Lady-Slipper
      dark maroon
          of Wake-Robin.
This
is a place
where stillness reigns,
but for the phoebe, over
and over ratcheting its name,
here, in lair of wolf and bear
where uneasy secrets toss under cover.
I linger in the spring woods of my origin,
inquire of this ancient fertile quietude
just where the meaning lies,
      and where
         the sacrifice.
Then
high, high
overhead, soft honking
of snow-geese recalls me, guides me
back through mottled light
to pared rock, where
far above in the *V*
a waving tail
of memory
trails.

BURNISHED

Your memory, green gold
inlaid in metal and stone of my bones,
holding me—the weight of it—yet
thoughts wander in upper stories of trees,

anastomosis of limbs
where gold and green flutter,
ready to ascend September gusts:
sun-catchers in the mandala of a tree,
in the round open-grown oak that unfolds
to parting skies, to light that streams
through summer thunder-bursts.

Thoughts of you, burnished anew
each day, ancient alchemy
deep in the pores of my bones.

PIS ALLER

Tears of the way—
in the unimpeded, we find composure:
release in letting be.

On the forest's edge
a sugar maple stands, rooted
in tattered fringe of isolation,
saps draining deep into December,
mosses dangling from the grain
of its northern face. Rains

that allow the driving winds
from the west, that allow
banishment, press themselves
into the skin of the tree:
it enfolds in overlapping layers
and warm shades of gray.

And the wind settles, retrieves
words from their meanings,
tunes to the clarity of air
and watches a flock of afterthoughts.
Arms of the tree feel them,
hold them, care for them.

All winter long
the world is askew:
constellations rise and fall
in the pure negative, black on white.

By early spring, everything
has changed and given way.

PACHELBEL'S HOPE
(On the Way to the Hospital)

I

Tires roll in muffled propulsion. Snow
bursts the bonds of cold and flies apart
before my eyes, silencing even my breath.
The car, myself, we grow hulls withholding
the progression of slow white—
long vowels that spread like silk, twilling
into the gibberish of my mind.

From a small coppice where in the dusk
wilted leaves gesture underside-up,
a sudden flush of larks—snow buntings—
startles with a piping,
sharp-whistled *teer, teer, teer, tears.*
Stillness again, wisps of remembering curl,
a silver frieze upon the windshield.

In feverish sleep you stir,
shift a small hand to my lap.
Only yesterday you played the flute,
Canon in D, every note an "O".
I spill out of myself, slip into a mute space,
the simplicity of listening.
Before me strains the strange geometry of sound.

II

Overcome by notes of your flute
that flood the road,
I reach past thronging thought,
press the ON knob for your festival audio:
the music rises from vestigial wells,
overlays my ruminant mind,
opens up drifts and flying snow—

a rich burst of midsummer,
warm flush of color—rose-bone
that melds, then swells
with laying-down of memory, recedes
with a sucking-back of sound—revisions
whirling notions and the snow
sticking round a portabella imprint
that opens to the road.

OFFERING TO THE UNSEEN

Kneeling
before the stone-altar
        I place on it these things:

a pollen fossil; a scrap
of three-and-a-half twill linen
water-stained and frayed;
a silver locket, tarnished,
fire-damaged; dry twigs
of shore-pine laid
layer upon layer; and atop all
a perfectly round pebble
from the shingle.

                Above,
hooked shawl of low-slung
tuckamore spreads, horizontal;
salt-dipped trunk
        and shorn roots
                straddle the rock.

Strike
of flint: a dance
as shadows spring
into red and blue tongues
that engulf.

MOTHER, GODDESS REAPING

Surge of joy and deep love urges me
to the cliff-edge where I lean, peering
beneath a jagged ledge into mysterious depths
      of my conception.

Inclined, drawn to fluid eyes
that roam in formidable chaos below,
I see each night-blue iris, still
within its swirl—the curdling foam
that collapses in cadence of low moans—
as rollers land with pound
      of metronome.

Sea-smocks spread and stretch
on tame-less waves receding, resurge
in roll and sway of ages. Bathed
in icy brine that upward flies
annihilating bounds of air and water,
I gaze through dazzling spray, swoon
to solemn swelling gutters
      of infernal yearning depths.

In drift and whoosh of wind, a seabird,
feathers flattened, wheels and banks its wings
before me and I reel back awash,
as the immense tireless sea
      changes her mind.

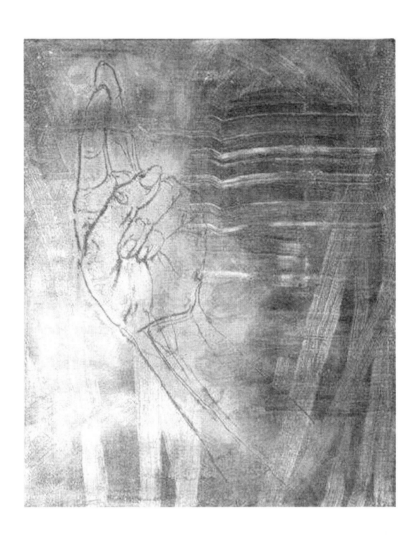

V

GATHERING STRANDS

ESSENCES

This unrelenting sadness, this
mountain of mortar bearing down
has birthed pure new things:

a perfect fern in moss-agate preserved;
smoldering glow in a lump of coal;
and forever treasured in amber amulet
a sweet honeybee embalmed.

*

So, what have we to do with grief?
Deeply pressed our memories live.
We have crept to the lip of the pit,
fingered dark essences, their secrets,
freed them from tangled roots.

Let us rise then, on coal-blue flames,
depart from age-old flyways, gather
air beneath our wings
and follow currents, merge
with things that quiver and shift.

BELLADONNA

In this dry summer, sizzling summer
of rememberings, I have found them:
the first blackberries, cool to my tongue,
hidden in filtered shade of maple.

Eager spines and clusters find my arms
and clutch, springing with golden-green
and reddish bursts of thirsty unripe fruit.
Beneath low branches hang the black ones,
the succulent ones, hiding reticent,
awaiting full term of sweetness.
See how strangely they grow—
double, misshapen, they cling
like fingers. Inseparable.

*

I recall co-joined infants,
surgeons couldn't free the pair:
they remain entwined
until one, or both are plucked.

*

And you and I, what of us?
Still twinned—your pain, my fear;
your blind groping hope
and my desire to stem the flow,

to heal as does the wild belladonna
that snakes its way between canes,
displaying a single teardrop berry—
homeopath amid the blackberries,
all about to swell with sudden rain.

GROUNDLING

When I was holding you,
I knew you were reaching
into the soil, for I saw
a smooth hazelnut split and grope
towards me, felt rootlets
from above touch my arms
as they grew
       through throbbing sod.

Where we touched, pain
swept in like water;
as a groundswell it flowed on
until gone. Nor was I afraid,
for there were air and light
and living things of every form,
shifting in shades of ochre
and chestnut that wove
       through warm black loam.

You were braver than I:
you did not wait for a savior,
stretched straight to the heart
of a god of heaven and earth
       with your roots.

BREATHING WATER

Walking beside myself,
tip-toeing over the duff,
bowing everywhere to earth,
I touch my own hand, the softness
of it—a suppleness undisturbed
by the true or false
between us.
             River

of a thousand glimmering eyes
twines through filtered slough-forest depths,
the seen and the unseen ever merging,
islands floating in umber
of still tannin waters.
Reflected in ox-bow of sluggish flow:
maple and flowering dogwood,
old growth oak, and on a knoll
some pine, all reaching
with a longing, their fingers
giving and taking all.

A gust, and leaves scutter
with raucous leave-taking
of a flock of grackles,
their drain-pipe notes and gurgles
sinking into pools below

where by chance I glimpse
a single beet-red dragonfly
resting upon a float of leaves
its wings invisible,
disclosed only by the veins.

These veins
that meander, remember
barely aware wringings known only
to the caress of my hand
and the inwardness of my hearing.
And in the throat a moan withheld,
trebled by the echo of its own emptiness.

But I am here,
leading myself into the water,
trusting that somehow long ago
I may have learned how to float,
to drift in and out of these places of exile

until I find myself again
in the shallows,
                alone
with the unnamed and the invisible,
fearless presences who whisper
that all grief is fleeting,
a falling away
                of debris

CALL-NOTE

You balance on a blade of grass
a ground-nesting sparrow, longing
for response to your song.
Nothing matters, only
the far-off call, an occasional
                              low note.

Distance devours sound,
throws a veil over the laying hold of it.
Muffled essences multiply, possess,
pin you in their webs, just
when you think
                    you might fly.

Listen. Listen.
Spoken in unknown language
a few words drift in. Perhaps
dissolution of sound
is something
                    of subsumption.

                    Yet
you flit from blade to stem to daisy,
drench yourself in illusions
of yellow pollen, sway
in the waiting, straining ever
for the clear call-note,
                         for perceptible reply.

BETWEEN

(you have parted the air between my thoughts
thrown open memory
a mute space before you came)

(between the notes of your minstrelsy
I slip through the moment that separates
a breath in, a breath out)

over small falls
I find myself carried
water above
                    sky beneath

a diaspore on froth
a million cilia twitching for air
a place to lodge
(somewhere between river and bank
of sonorous hollow below)

FINAL FLIGHT

Wings lie lightly in your lap:
hands clasped, entwined at the webs,
fingers open—a butterfly-moth
waiting for the candle or advent
of a banshee wailing through limbs
of the jumping-tree by the creek.

A tingling as damp tips unfold,
then flight into the fire-fly
night, powdery wing-eyes
pale reflections of the moon
upon water.
        Fly,

fly into the flames of leaves
and cattails in the shallows, or
find your way to a lone milkweed
in the wet meadowlands, there to lay
in the crook of a stem
your many tales.

ABOUT THE AUTHOR

To know Marina, you have only to meet her children, build a house with her husband, run a white river with her friends, touch a dying client; you could hike the North Cayuga Slough Forest, wander in her gardens or stand before one of her paintings.

This is Marina's first book. Her work has been published by Main Street, Tower Poetry Society, and Seasons (now On Nature) and her environmental column has been carried by multiple newpapers.

Marina is a graduate of McMaster University's Certificate of Writing program.

Marina is currently working on two other books: a children's book, which includes translations of a few of her grandmother's tales; and a series of stories conceived during years on the road as a home care therapist.

VALE IN THE DUNES

Slowly sinking into the friable soil
of having been, like sand in an hourglass
that leaves no presence.

The landscape answers my call:
something rises beneath me,
finally I meet myself.

Here in these dunes,
kneeling in a small green vale
I become the things I've cared for.

YOU MAY TOUCH THIS POEM
IT IS A STONE

She sits
polishing a rose-stone, gazes
into it, sees only her own eyes, keeps
searching for something insoluble that lives
therein. Some thought, some spirit of the dead.
An animal. A deep secret scavenged from dreams.
Equanimity. Patience. Approbation of stone grows
in her. Anguish has scoured away the surface.
Thus eroded and round she finds it in her
hands, this stone absently retrieved
from the riverbed.

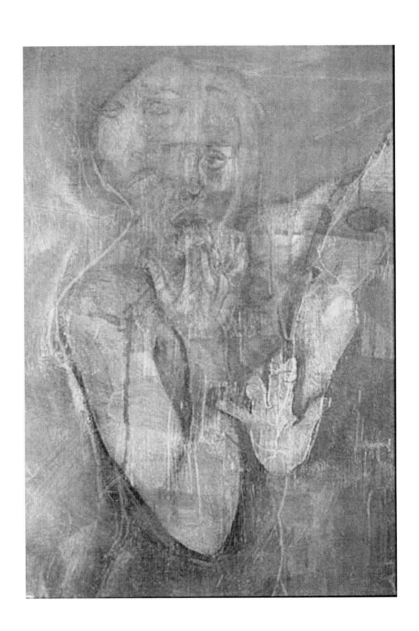

ARTIST'S STATEMENT

I close my eyes during the act of creating. Before a canvas pregnant with paint, I lay bare, with slightly sprawled fingers, the emerging image of a head.

As I feel the figure, it becomes foreign. It fills with distinct dimensions and depths, creases and curves. The form and the effect of its ambience are sensed with one hand, and concurrently conveyed to be carved into paint with the other. I temper my touch to both listen and speak.

I call my technique Blind-Touch Contouring.

Blindness is a condition often mystified by means of metaphor or perceived in a lamentable light. As it happens, it holds its own innate vision, independence and will to interpret the world. Each of us is calmed by its coming moment as we close our eyes to dream, or sit in the darkness to contemplate. By spying inwards, we tend to an expectant terrain of touch tuned with inner imagery, taste, sound and smell. Blindness is a seabed of synthesis, offering insight, a sixth sense.

It is intuition, after all, and the memory of veiled marvels, that implores me to express via the gift of visual sensation, yet refrain from relying on its facility. I respectfully stir a state of sightlessness to welcome the awareness touch entrusts to my art.

Every infant enters life with the initial and essential experience of plying fingers. The hand naturally intuits and translates with uncanny vividness. In view of this, my painting incarnates a nascent visuality as it is nurtured by touch and birthed beneath closed lids.

Laura Dawn Fernando

CPSIA information can be obtained at www.ICGtesting.com
Printed in the USA
LVOW080912300812

296559LV00001B/37/P